MIND RENEWAL

The
Doorway
To

VICTORIOUS
LIVING

**How To Develop
The Mindset For A Triumphant Life**

By Phillip Woods

This Is A Publication of

Take Charge Enterprises, Inc.

MIND RENEWAL THE DOORWAY TO VICTORIOUS LIVING

PREVIOUSLY ENTITLED: VICTORIOUS LIVING THROUGH BIBLICAL MIND RENEWAL

ISBN 1-4243-0321-4
Copyright 1995
Revised: 2016

Published by, Cover & Text Design
Take Charge Enterprises, Inc.

Printed in the United States of America.

PREFACE

The intent of this book, is to show you how to live a life, of victory over every obstacle, adversity and mental roadblocks to success, wellbeing and prosperity, by exploring the principles of renewing the mind, and how to use them. As well as, how to break unproductive habits, through the process of Biblical Meditation.

Mind Renewing, is not something that takes place over night. It is a process that takes time, effort, perseverance and determination. The purpose for Biblical mind renewal, is to cause ones thoughts, vernacular and behavior, to come into agreement with God's Word. It means; to come to a place, wherein you begin to think as God thinks, see as God sees, and speak as God speaks. Biblical mind renewal, is the process that has to take place, in a believer's life, in order to change or renew, their way of thinking, from the way they thought, before he or she became a child of God.

As you increase in the knowledge of God's word, and spend time meditating on what you have learned, you began the first phase of empowering yourself, to live a victorious Christian life. You will also come to a place of understanding, how to apply that knowledge to your life for positive results. It is said, "knowledge is power." But I say, "knowledge is potential power." Because what we know, empowers us, only when we put to practice the information we have ascertained. This is the only way we can accomplish, and enjoy, all that God has intended for us, individually and as a Body of believers.

We, as Christians, according to Romans 12:2, should not think or speak the same as the world system, which is governed by Satan. Romans 12:2 says,

"...be not conformed to this world: but be ye transformed by the renewing of your mind, that ye may prove what is that good, and acceptable, and perfect will of God."

In other words, God has a system as well, which is in contrast to the world's system. This is what Jesus was referring to, when he said, "...but seek yea first the Kingdom of God, and all these things shall be added unto you." As we follow the ways of God, and the leading of the Holy Spirit, we will ultimately, experience His best for our lives.

There are many books written on how to obtain happiness and peace of mind, however, only God knows how such a state of being is accomplished. It is only when we begin to live under His government and authority, will we enjoy true happiness, peace of mind and success.

There is a verse of scripture, I like to reflect on from time to time.

Acquaint now thyself with Him, and be at peace,
thereby good shall come unto thee..
I really like the amplified bible's version.

Acquaint now thyself with Him, [agree with God and
show yourself to be conformed to His will] and be at
peace; by that [you shall prosper and great] good
shall come to you.

Wow, this verse, in a nutshell, says as we conform to God's way of doing things, prosperity and good, **SHALL COME TO US.**

The way of the world is fear, lust, greed, pride, self exhortation, worry, failure, death, lack, etc., which are all contrary to the Word and will of God for his children. Consequently, many people were raised under the influences of many of these conducts, if not all of them.

Consider this, if a person is forty years old, before he is born again, he would have experienced forty years of thinking, speaking and seeing things contrary to the word and will of God. Therefore, this person has at least thirty-five years of bad thinking, beliefs and convictions that he has to change.

The longer you think a certain way, the harder it is to change, just as, the longer you behave a certain way, or the longer a certain habit exists in your life, the longer it may take to break it. So you must understand, mind renewing is necessary, but it could take a considerable amount of time and effort, if change is to come in ones life. Nevertheless, regardless to how long you have thought or behaved a certain way, the word of God instructs you to renew your mind.

Therefore, it is possible to make such a mental and ultimately physical change. However, you will have to apply the principles that are outlined in this book, as well as, additional information the Holy Spirit reveals to you during your studies.

Jesus said in the book of John the 8th chapter verses 31 & 32,

"If you continue in my word, then are ye my disciples indeed; And ye shall know the truth, and the truth shall make you free."

The only way a person can be made free is by a change of mind, a renewing of the mind. The scriptures are not referring to the conscious mind, but the inner mind, the mind of your spirit, or the subconscious mind. We don't speak much of the subconscious mind, especially from the pulpit, nevertheless, that is the mind that needs to be renewed. It is there where a man's beliefs and convictions are established, based on his previous experiences, teachings and up bringing.

When you were born again, Jesus set you free from the power of sin and death, and the authority of Satan. Such freedom is spiritual and positional. You have this liberty through Jesus Christ, however, in order to live the new life, your mind must be renewed to it, by spending time in study and meditation of the word of God.

Remember, for years we have been programmed, so to speak, through information, experiences and influences.

However, you are now a new creature, for it is written;

Therefore If any man be in Christ, he is a new creature: old things are passed away; behold, all things are become new. II Cor. 5:17
And you live in another Kingdom.

.
...Who hast delivered us from the powers of darkness, and hast translated us into the kingdom of his dear son. Col. 1:13

That being the case, we must now learn to govern our lives, according to this new kingdom.

I was once reading a book, entitled, "Drawing nigh unto God". After reading a few pages, I looked up to God and said, "God I need to draw nearer to you," I thought he would be pleased with that! However, he immediately responded by saying, "you can't get any closer to me then you are." He said, "we are one, you are in me and I'm in you. What you must do is draw closer in your thought life, you must change your way of thinking by thinking in line with my word."

Mind renewal is the most important thing to give priority to, now that you are a citizen of the kingdom. You must think like God thinks, and keep His word in your mouth, so you can prove His will to your family, friends and the world around you.

People need to know, that the kingdom of God has come, however, the only way this is going to happen, is through you and I, as we live a victorious, successful and prosperous life through Christ Jesus, by applying the principles of mind renewal, which are found in this book.

Ruth and I encourage you to listen carefully to the Holy Spirit as you read. Be Fruitful & Multiply.

Table of Contents

Summary & Overview
4 Steps To Renewing The Mind

NEXT LEVEL MINISTRIES

INTERNATIONAL
AKA: PHILLIP WOODS MINISTRIES
(803) 348-0882
Email : pwoods1204@gmail.com
Website : phillipwoodsministries.com
©Copyright 1995; Revised 2016
Published By
Take Charge Enterprises, Inc., Columbia, SC
(803) 348-0882

Chapter 1

Mind Renewing:

Changing The Way You Think

Chapter One

Changing The Way You Think

Before you start this chapter, I want you to take a few minutes to think about, how you think of yourself. Think about all that pertains to you. Well, what do you think? Do you like the way you think of and see yourself? It is written "as a man thinketh in his heart, so is he", and of course, the way you think of yourself is also the way you will see yourself. Believe it or not, you are the sum total of your thoughts, you are what you think you are, nothing more and nothing less.

There are many different reasons why we may think a certain way. Our surroundings, our past, our experiences, whether good or bad, and what we are constantly hearing about ourselves, from other people, can all play a big part, in the way we think and see ourselves.

Perhaps your surroundings are very humiliating, where poverty and lack are the norm; perhaps many of the people who are around you, have a very low self-image and self-esteem about themselves, and the only picture that anyone ever paints for you, is one of failure and worthlessness. Primarily, this is the kind of environment I grew up in.

I remember a coach at the high school I attended, who had a very negative perception and stigma about the young men that grew up in my community. This coaches' point of view, concerning the guys from my neighborhood, was one he voiced often. He would say, "only thugs and worthless people came from where we lived," although, there were some very talented, young men and women among us. However, unfortunately, many thought of and saw themselves in the same way this coach saw them.

It is a sad thing, when people allow themselves to accept another person's negative point of view of them, and be pressured into being and thinking in the same negative way.

God has given each of us, distinct personalities, with special individual qualities and capabilities, to achieve whatever we set our hearts and minds to. If we are consumed by trying to think, act or be like someone else, we will never fulfill our purpose in life. That is, whatever we desires to do that amounts to good and is beneficial for oneself and others.

Maybe you have had some very traumatic situations to occur in your past, that has much to do with the way you think about yourself today. For instance, you may have been a victim of a rape or child molestation, or you may have been imprisoned or rejected by loved ones for some reason or another. Perhaps you've been fired or laid off from a job, after having given your very best to the company for many years. In any case, these and many past events could be governing the way you think of yourself today. Whatever the case may be in your situation, I want you to consider very carefully what I am about to share with you.

The day you were born again, at that very moment you began a new life. Your spiritual nature and your identity were immediately changed, regardless to whatever else remained the same around you. In 2 Corinthians 5:17, Paul said,

"therefore, if any man be in Christ he is a new creature: old things are past away; behold all things are become new."

Paul also said in his letter to the Philippians, chapter 3, verse 13,

"Brethren, I count not myself to have apprehended: but this one thing I do, forgetting those things which are behind and reaching forth unto those things which are before."

You must take Paul's example and forget those negative things that you experienced in your past, and look to the future with expectant hope of better things, and press forward.

The word "forget" in Philippians 3:13 means; **to be unable to recall** (*something previously known*) **to the mind; it means to fail to or cease to remember.**

This is and will always be an intentional act of ones will. It will not happen automatically. You will have to make a conscious and deliberate decision to forget and press on, not to remember any more the hurts, disappointments and the bad experiences that happened in your past.

When you were born again, you became a new creature, a new being in Christ, therefore, regardless to what has happened to you or what you have done, it has been blotted out by the blood of Jesus. The old you, was crucified with Christ Jesus. You must remember, it doesn't matter what type of lifestyle you led prior to your new birth, God, by and through the blood of Jesus, has cleansed you He has forgiven you, and forgotten your past. Now you must also forget it, and come to a place of forgiving yourself, for all past sin and disappointments, as well as others, who have wronged you. You must go on with your life and enjoy it to the fullest. With great expectation of exciting, victorious and successful years to come.

We, as children of God, have been instructed by God, through His written word, to think a certain way. Notice what Philippians 4:8 says....

"Finally, brethren, whatsoever things are true, whatsoever things are honest, whatsoever things are just, whatsoever things are pure, whatsoever things are lovely, whatsoever things are of a good report; if there be any virtue, and if there be any praise, think on these things."

Therefore, if we do not think as God says we ought to, we are rebelling and disobeying Him. Go with me to James 1:22, here we read…
"but be ye doers of the word, and not hearers only, deceiving your own selves."

Notice if you will, in this scripture, James warns us not to be hearers ONLY of God's word, but we are to be doers also, otherwise, we are deceiving and depriving ourselves of the good life Jesus died to give us.

When you look into the scriptures and you see what God is saying about you as His child, it is your responsibility to behave yourself in accordance to what God has said. However, it will be totally impossible for you to act or behave the way God requires, until you begin to think and see yourself as He thinks of and sees you. Be mindful, this can only be done through the process of renewing the mind, making God's thoughts your thoughts. Check out this promise.

For my thoughts are not your thoughts, neither are your ways my ways, saith the Lord. For as the heavens are higher than the earth, so are my ways higher than your ways and my thoughts than your thoughts. For as the rain cometh down, and the snow from heaven, and returneth not thither, but watereth the earth, and maketh it bring forth and bud, that it may give seed to the sower, and bread to the eater: So shall my word be that goeth forth out of my mouth: it shall not return unto me void , but it shall accomplish that which I please, and it shall prosper in the thing whereto I sent it. For ye shall go out with joy, and be led forth with peace: the mountains and the hills shall break forth before you into singing, and all the trees of the field shall clap their hands. Instead of the thorn shall come up the fir tree, and instead of the brier shall come up the myrtle tree: and it shall to the Lord for a name, for an everlasting sign that shall not be cut off. Is. 55:8-13

This is the promise of the good life as a result of renewing our minds to the word of God.

Look carefully at what Paul says in the book of Romans 12:1-2 "I beseech you therefore, brethren, by the mercies of God, that you present your bodies a living sacrifice, holy, acceptable unto God, which is your reasonable service. And be not conformed to this world: but be ye transformed, by the renewing of your mind, that you may prove what is that good and acceptable, and perfect will of God."

In verse two, Paul says, we are not to be dictated by the world system as unbelievers are, who are constantly governed by the prince of the air, and the powers of darkness. We are not to be overwhelmed by fear, hatred, lust, greed and every evil work. But our lives, as children of God, are to be governed by the Word of God.

Paul gives us the impression that at one point in life, we were also ruled by these same fleshly behaviors, when he said, we were to be transformed or changed. Paul goes on to indicate that the only way we are going to be changed is by the renewing of our minds. Only then, will we be able to demonstrate to the world, what is the perfect and acceptable will of God for all of mankind.

Agreeing With God

"Acquaint now thyself with him, and be at peace: thereby good shall come unto thee"
(Job 22:21)

The word acquaint has a dual meaning in this particular text. First, it means *to familiarize yourself with someone or thing;* and secondly, it means *to agree with or to come into an agreement with*.

Now in this case, the scripture is saying we are to familiarize ourselves with God, and come into agreement with Him. Or we could say it this way, look into the Word of God and see what He is saying about you, your circumstances, marriage, finances etc. and then agree with Him in every way; in your thoughts, speech and actions.

Think of yourself in the same way God sees you. Speak of yourself the same way God speaks of you. Stop fighting against Him, and come into agreement with what He has said about you. Do not speak or think of yourself and circumstances contrary to His word. By agreeing with God, the scriptures says... Good shall come unto thee, and He shall, by the power of the Holy Spirit change your situation.

You see, God has already given us His Son to make up the difference between us and Himself, so we can become the partakers of His divine nature. Now the responsibility is on us to renew our minds so that the way we think will line up with God's Word.

Let's look at an example from the Old Testament of how God was highly displeased with His people, even to the point of allowing them to die in the wilderness, having not received the promised benefits, all because of the way they saw and spoke of themselves, which was contrary to what God had spoken about them.

It says, "and they went and came to Moses, and to Aaron, and to all the congregation of the children of Israel, unto the wilderness of Paran, to Kadesh; and brought back word unto them, and unto all the congregation, and showed them the fruit of the land. And they told him and said,

"we came unto the land wither thou sentest us, and surely it floweth with milk and honey; and this is the fruit of it. Nevertheless, the people be strong that dwell in the land, and the cities are walled, and very great: and moreover we saw the children of Anak there. The amalekites dwell in the land of the south: and the Hittites, and the Jebusites, and the Amorites, dwell in the mountains: and the Canaanites dwell by the sea, and by the coast of Jordan. And Caleb stilled the people before Moses, and said, let us go up at once and possess it; FOR WE ARE WELL ABLE TO OVERCOME IT. But the men that went up with him said, We be not able to go up against the people for they are stronger then we.

And they brought up an evil report of the land… and all the people that we saw in it are men of great stature. And there WE SAW THE GIANTS, the sons of Anak, which come of the giants: and WE WERE IN OUR OWN SIGHT AS GRASSHOP-PERS, and so were we in their sight". (Numbers 13:26-33)

Mind you, God had already told them that the land belonged to them, nevertheless, they said, "they were unable to take it because they saw themselves as "grasshoppers" among the giants." They did not agree with God, who said, "they were well able to possess the land," He had already given them.

Consequently, they all died outside of the land that flowed with milk and honey with the exception of those that said they were well able to do those things that God already said they could do.

Only by reading and searching the scriptures for yourself, will you discover all of what God has said concerning you. The bible tells us that God says, "you can do all things through Christ who strengthens or empowers you," therefore, you should never say, you can not do whatever He said you can do.

God says He is with you, then you should never say you are alone. God says you are strong, then you are never to say you are weak. He says you are rich, there-fore never say, you are poor or broke. God says, you are healed, never, ever say you are sick… **DO YOU GET THE POINT?**

By knowing for yourself, the truth of God's Word, about all that concerns you, the peace of God that passes all understanding, will be with you; As well as, the power of the Holy Spirit, working within you, empowering you, to be all that God said you are, by the renewing of your mind.

Overcoming Self

I remember when the Lord spoke to me concerning habits that some Christians have, such as smoking, excessive drinking or viewing pornography. He said, "often times people say, "that person has a nicotine, alcohol or a lusting demon operating in their lives." But on the contrary, what the person has is a bad habit that has not yet been broken". *(We will deal more with this in chapter five)*

Yes, I do believe there are Christians who have problems with old stubborn habits, although, they are already born again and filled with the Spirit. You may ask, how could that be? Recall to mind, the statement that Paul made in Romans 12:1-2, he said, **YOU** are to present **YOUR OWN** body a living sacrifice and **YOU** are to renew **YOUR OWN** mind. When a person gets saved, the initial change that takes place in their lives,, has taken place on the inside. It is the spirit of the person that is born again. However, nothing happens to his mind nor his body, until he renews his mind with the Word of God. This is why we have a personal responsibility, to change the way we think and act, after the new birth.

Nevertheless, there are some people who, even after being born again, have not been able to bring their mind and body, under subjection to their new self, and to the Word of God, in certain areas of their lives. Because of this, they continue to walk in the old habits, the old nature that they walked in, before the new birth.

At the age of around 12 or 13 years old I started using drugs. I went from smoking pot to popping speed to shooting bams, before the Lord saved me. The drugs, I got over immediately, but there was another habit I had picked up at an early age, which took me years to kick, it was viewing pornography. It was during my major struggle with pornography, when the Holy Spirit begin teaching me about mind renewal through biblical meditation, which is what inspired this book.

I had been fasting and praying (on and off) for approximately 40 days, trying to break the habit, when my mother mentioned to me that a man of God was coming to town. He was from New Jersey, but his name was becoming a household name here, among the Pentecostal.

She suggested that I go and have him pray for me, which I agreed to. I was the first person to get to the place of the meeting, I mean, I was there before they opened the doors.

I waited patiently through all of the accolades, awards and presentations, the preaching of the word and finally the alter call.

I was up there front and center. The speaker started to my left, as he laid hands on those that were there for prayer, emotions went wild. They were dancing, shouting, speaking in tongues and falling on the floor. I knew that when he was to lay hands on me, the power of God was going to take control.

Finally he got to me. I stretched my hands toward heaven with great expectation, only to feel his hand on my head. I felt absolutely nothing but his hand. He said a few words and went to the next person. As I stood there disappointed, I heard the voice of the Holy Spirit gently ask me, "what are you doing here"? I quickly responded by saying, "Lord you know why I'm here". He then said to me, "go home and break your fast." I left right then, while the man of God was still praying for others, for I had heard from the Lord. I remember stopping at a convenient store and bought myself two hot dogs and a grape soda, man was I glad to end that fast. Shortly after that, the Holy Spirit begin to teach me the principles of meditation and how to break that habit of pornography viewing. These principles can be applied to any kind of habit or the renewing of your mind in any area as you practice them. We will dig deeply into them later.

Notice what Paul says in 1 Corinthians 6:12

"I can do anything I want to, if Christ has not said no, but some of these things are not good for me.

Even if I am allowed to do them, I'll refuse to, if I think they might get such a grip on me that I cannot easily stop when I want to. " (the Living Bible):

Also 1Corinthians 9:27(KJV) says,

"but I keep under MY body, and bring it into subjection..."

Notice very carefully what Paul is saying when he says.... **I** keep under **MY BODY!!** You see, man is made of three parts. Man is Spirit, he has a Soul or Mind, and he lives in a Body. The **I** that Paul is referring to in this passage of scripture is the spirit man. The spirit man is struggling to keep his body under subjection from the control and appetites of the flesh.

Now the mind is the control center of all bodily activity. The problem is not primarily your body that you are having trouble with, but it is your mind. Control your mind and you will control your body, which is the same as self-discipline or to have temperance. Self-discipline begins in the mind, not the body.

Therefore, when a habit is formed (good or bad) it is first formed in the mind. The pattern of thought and desires that dominate the mind, will also dominate your behavior. That is why the scripture says... *as a man thinketh (that is, continues to think) so is he.*

If you constantly think you must have a particular thing to satisfy you, such as cigarettes, strong drinks, excessive sex, etc.; your body and behavior will continue to be dominated by the thoughts and desire that you constantly think on.

But on the other hand, if you can change the way you think and recognize that you **Do Not HAVE To HAVE IT**, then you are on your way to breaking that particular habit.

The Greatest Challenge

"Success Requires That You Push Yourself Beyond Your Comfort Zone"

The greatest challenge to succeeding at anything, is the challenge of overcoming one's self. You are the one who is ultimately responsible for your failing or succeeding in any giving endeavor. You will be your greatest liability or your greatest asset.

You must fix your mind on a particular goal or desire, and maintain that fixation until it is completed. Once you have become mentally disciplined, on a set course, nothing or no one can stop you from succeeding, not even Satan.

Nevertheless, you must constantly push yourself, you have to master the art of self motivation, and autosuggestion. In other words you have to do all you can to convince yourself of your ability to bring about the desired change.

Don't allow yourself to settle, for accepting something, that does not attribute to you being a successful and productive individual, as well as, a good representative of the Kingdom of our God.

When you make that, no turning back, kind of a decision and remain determined, it is a done deal. Even if you were to fall short from time to time you won't give up, because you have made up your mind. When the mind is made up, you will keep coming back or getting up until you win.

Now I know for a fact, and by personal experience, it is easier said than done. But, I also know, if you persevere in the principles of Biblical Mind Renewal, your desired change will come.

Another thing I have had to change in my personal life, was the image of lack or nor having enough. Lack was also a self portrait I had of myself while at an early age. My mother and father had me and eight other children to provide for. My dad worked as a trash truck driver for the City of Columbia. My mom did odd jobs; house cleaning, sitting with the elderly, and working at a day care center, to name a few. We Lived in the projects, received government assistance, that is food stamps and the food supply.

About three times a year, my father would bring home huge Gaylord size boxes of clothing. His trash truck would be filled with boxes of every type of clothing we needed, from under wear to outer wear, shoes, socks, jackets and coats. We would go through the boxes, collecting all we needed, then my mother would call the neighbors over so they could get what they wanted. Although we had what we needed, as far as clothing was concern, we never could seem to keep up with our rent payment or purchase much of anything with cash.

At a young age, this image of lack, was instilled into my inner consciousness. It was like a seed planted in me that grew over the years, and when I got married with responsibilities of my own, I struggled with the lack mentality. I did not realize how much the lack image within me was actually governing my thoughts, thus governing my finances. As long as I maintained a, we don't have enough mentality, I was creating an environment that seemed to manifest what I constantly meditated on, which was lack. Although I was a hard worker, a faithful tithe worshiper, generous giver to those in need and took my bill paying responsibilities seriously, it seemed as though, we just couldn't rise above not having enough.

It wasn't until the Holy Spirit started teaching me about what had happened years ago and what was currently happening, that I begin to understand what I was doing to myself by allowing my mind to meditate on the thought of not having enough. It was not easy getting started, neither has it been easy maintaining a change of mind where lack and or prosperity is concern.

Mind renewing is said to be the most laborious form of work a Christian will have to perform. It is constant work to keep your mind focus on a particular way of thinking when everything around you contradicts those thoughts. For instance, holding onto a more than enough mindset, or a wealthy and prosperous consciousness, when there seems to never be enough. It is said that wealth, success and prosperity has to start within a person before he will begin to see outward evidence of it. Of course, this could be considered true when we think of it in light of the scripture which says, "as a man thinketh, or habitually thinks, so is he.

Therefore, if I always think of myself as a failure then I'll always be defeated, if I think I can't do it then I will never succeed at it. It seems easier to think negatively then it does positive. That is because of all the negative energy around us in this negative world system that we live in. So it takes work, diligence and persistence to keep your inner world or inner consciousness in line with God's kingdom until it is manifested for you. Without any shame or excuse, I must admit, I'm still at work. However, my labor will not be in vain, how about yours.

Chapter 2

Mind Renewing:

Changing The Way You See YOURSELF

What you are constantly seeing or observing, can weigh heavily, upon the pattern of thoughts that goes through your mind. As I have already stated, your thoughts will determine your behavior.

When God reveals something to you, that which is revealed, is full of life. It has the ability to bring itself to pass. Just like a seed has in it, the power to produce that which is inside. You don't have to make it grow, it just grows. However, it has to be planted of course. The same must be done with the revelation or image God gives to you. It has to be embraced and believed, no matter how impossible it may seem. If God showed it to you, it is like a seed that has the ability to produce on it's own, it will bring itself to pass, if you keep it planted in your heart.

Satan works in the opposite. He is trying to plant his seeds of negativism, using the power of vexation. Vexation occurs, when someone is constantly seeing and or hearing something that is negative. To vex means; to wear down mentally or oppress. Satan bombards your mind with thoughts and images, that opposes what God has shown you. He is very persistent. He is attempting to wear you down mentally, until you give in to what he is saying. He knows if he can get you to accept it, then it to, like the promises of God will be planted in your heart, begin to grow, and come to pass. However, only one seed can come to pass, what Satan is saying or what God has revealed to you.

Only you can determine which one will come to pass. The one you accept and believe is the one that will bear fruit.

In 2 Peter 2:7,8 we see, that it was what Lot constantly saw and heard, among the people of Sodom and Gomorrah, that caused him to be "vexed": which means; to wear down mentally or oppress. What Lot constantly saw and heard, weighed heavily upon his mind, which kept his mind subject to thinking a certain way.

Here's the way it is actually written in the scriptures

....And delivered just Lot, vexed with the filthy conversation of the wicked: (For that righteous man dwelling among them, in seeing and hearing, vexed his righteous soul from day to day with their unlawful deeds;)

Although the scriptures, do not give specific evidence, that Lot actually indulged in the perversions of Sodom and Gomorrah, nevertheless, his way of thinking could have caused him to behave ungodly. The scriptures does, however, allows us to see, how Lot was hesitant to leave the city, even though, the Angels of the Lord, told him of God's intentions to destroy it.

There was something going on inside of him, that caused him to wrestle with the fact that God was about to destroy the city.

Here, we see that the Angels had to take Lot by the hand and lead him out of the city, because he would not turn and leave on his own.

Do you think, perhaps his flesh was warring against his spirit? Have you ever experience your flesh at war against your spirit? If you are honest, you know it happens more than you would want to admit, or talk about.

I mentioned earlier, about my addiction to porn. One day, while on my job sight, I came across a magazine, boy did I struggle, with the idea of keeping it or throwing it away. My flesh was warring against my spirit. I'm telling you, all kinds of thoughts and images was bombarding my mind, trying to suppress me, so I wouldn't do the right thing. Although my spirit won the battle, as I forced myself to throw it away, but when I did, I kid you not, I wanted to cry. That is how much my flesh wanted to keep that magazine.

I believe Lot was experiencing something very similar. It seems as though, he wrestled with the need to go with the angles and a desire to follow those fleshly impulses, to stay in the city.

What you see, on a constant basis, can influence you, much quicker, than what you hear. We all have heard the saying, a picture is worth a thousand words.

In conclusion to all you've read thus far, what you see, hear and say will ultimately determine what you will do and or become.

Therefore, what kind of picture have you painted of yourself? Keep in mind, the way you view yourself, through your own eyes or through the eyes of others, will play a vital part in how you carry yourself. Your perception of yourself is an important factor in your attitude toward yourself and others. For instance, if you see yourself as one who always fails, or as one who can't overcome certain habits, addictions or circumstances, then you're subject to never put forth the necessary effort, to accomplish victory in those areas.

If you look only at what is, then you will never obtain what can be. However, if you're willing to put forth the effort to change what you're seeing, then success is all most guaranteed.

In order to change any images you have accepted about yourself, especially those that are in contrast to God's word, you must master your thoughts and create new images. This is all scriptural of course, for instance, consider Rom. 12:2 which says,

"And be not conformed to this world : but be ye transformed by the renewing of your mind"...

Notice, the scripture says, we are not to act like the world or unbelievers, and we are to be transformed or changed of any behavior that contradicts the kingdom of God, by the renewing of our minds.

Here's another, 11 Cor. 10:5 says,

"Casting down <u>imaginations</u>, and every high thing that exalts itself against the knowledge of God, and bringing into captivity every <u>thought</u> into the obedience of Christ".

Notice here, Paul says, we have to deal with our imaginations and thoughts. He said in Romans 12, we must renew the mind, however, that which rules the mind and eventually governs our behavior, stems from the root of our thoughts and imaginations.

If what you see, is not what you want for your future, then you must change what you are looking at and or thinking about. **Think about, what you are thinking about.** What type of thoughts dominates your thinking the most, negative ones or thoughts which lines up with God's word?

The One thing you must practice, is looking into the word of God, so you can see what you truly looks like. Consider this, how did the first man know, he was a man, he had never seen a man before. Left alone, he could have thought , man was a duck. God the creator told him what he was. He said. *"Let us make man in our image".* He called him man before He created him, then taught him who he was, and what he was responsible for. He did the same with the woman.

So it is today, only God the creator, knows our true identity, for he is the one who gave it to us.

The way we realize it today, is by looking into his word, to see what he has said about us. Let's look at a couple of scriptures from the book of James.

"But be ye doers of the word, and not hearers only, deceiving your own selves. For if any be a hearer of the word, and not a doer, he is like unto a man beholding his natural face in a glass: For he beholdeth himself, and go his way, and straightway forgetteth what manner of man he was". James 1:22-24

James is simply saying, we must look into the word of God, to see what it says about us and then act like it, therefore, however the scriptures describes a man to be, it is how a man or woman should act. The identity of a man and woman is clearly revealed in the bible , there is no room for error. There is no description for a homosexual or lesbian, that is, a man acting like a woman or a woman acting like a man. I have heard it said, a man should get in touch with his feminine side. When I heard that, I immediately pointed at the woman, for she is the feminine side of the man. She is the woman who was taken out of man. She is the man with a womb, (wo`man) breasts and all of her innate sensual behaviors. Have you ever notice that a woman doesn't have to practice being a woman or sexy or sensuous, it just comes natural. However, a man, on the other hand, has to make himself act like a woman, because it doesn't come naturally, because it isn't natural. When a man looks into the word and see himself as he should be, and walks away, acting like a woman, he is deceiving himself. How can the created say to the creator, I'm not who you say I'm.

Here's another,

"But we all, with open face beholding as in a glass, the glory of the Lord, are changed into the same image, from glory to glory, even as, by the Spirit of the Lord".

The amplified version says it like this,

"And all of us, as with unveiled face, [because we] continue to behold [in the word of God] as in a mirror, the glory of the Lord, are constantly being transformed into his very own image, in ever increasing splendor and from one degree of glory unto another...

Looking into the word of God, reading and meditating on it, will impress upon your subconscious mind, the very image of that, which you are meditating on. If you keep reading and hearing the word, you will be empowered by the Holy Spirit, or should I say, the power of the Holy Spirit, working through the word, will bring about the transformation of thought and behavior that God intended in you.

The scripture says **_"all things are possible to him that believeth:_** believing in the ability of God is one thing, but you must also believe in your ability to accomplish what you desire.

You see, God does have a very important part to play in your success, however, He can not do His part, without your cooperation.

Eph. 3:20 says, "Now unto him that is able to do exceeding abundantly above all that we ask or think, according to the power that worketh in us.

Notice, the scripture says God is able, however, it is according to his power that is inside us. In order for that power to work, we must renew our minds to the scriptures, and walk by faith, not by sight or our senses.

First Things First

Therefore, come into agreement with what God has said about you. Paint a picture in your mind that lines up with what He says in His word.

Remember, you must take the time to find out what He said about every area of your life, that you want to change, then begin the process of change. It is only when you begin to see yourself as God sees you that you will begin to excel and demonstrate the God-given abilities to accomplish whatever you desire.

If God sees you as an over-comer, an achiever, more than a conqueror, strong and well able, but you see yourself totally opposite of what He sees in you, then your perspective of yourself, will lessen God's chances, of helping you become, what He has said concerning you. Remember, it is only when you begin to see yourself as God sees you, that you begin to excel and demonstrate, the God giving abilities, to accomplish or succeed at anything of value.

In our last chapter, we talked about how the Israelites deprived themselves of God's blessings, because of the way they thought of themselves. It was not only the way they thought of themselves, but also the way that they viewed themselves in their own eyes.

Remember, God told Moses to send twelve men to spy out the land that He had ALREADY given them. The bible tells us that they returned to Moses with an evil report. Let us look at Chapter 13 of Numbers, verse 33, it says...

"and there we saw the giants, the sons of Anak, which come of the giants: and WE WERE IN OUR OWN SIGHT AS GRASSHOPPERS, AND SO WE WERE IN THEIR SIGHT."

It is of utmost importance that we understand what is taking place here. It was because of the way they saw themselves that they missed out on the best that God had for them. Therefore, they never saw the full manifestation of the ability of God at work on their behalf. These people refused to cooperate with God, consequently, they ended up dying in the wilderness, deprived of the benefits of God, all because they saw themselves differently from the way God saw them.

God says, you are able, you are strong, you are capable. As you continuously see yourself the way God sees you, and begin to act that a way, then God with your cooperation, will cause you to prosper in all that you set your hands to.

God works in and through us, but we must agree with him, it is imperative that we align our thinking up with his thoughts. For how can two walk together unless they agree. God isn't going to change his ways for us. We must conform to them, he is the one who sets the standard.

Never speak of yourself or see yourself as a failure or a loser. Although, you may have failed in a particular endeavor, you must always maintain a positive image or picture in your mind, seeing yourself as one who is prevailing, victorious and triumphant through Jesus Christ, the author and finisher of your faith. You can not do that without constantly looking into the mirror (God's Word).

A lost is something which occurs in a moment of time, it is the result of an event, task or endeavor, not the identity of the individual (s) involved. You are created in the image of God, the very nature and life of him, inhabits you. You have bounce back ability. You are as buoyant as a ping pong ball in water, it never stays on the bottom, no matter how many times it is pushed down.

The word of God, is like a mirror you look into, to see yourself, the way you really are. God's word is the only true source of information that will show you your true identity, what you are capable of doing, and what you can rightfully have in life.

The scriptures says, *"therefore if any man be in Christ, he is a new creature: old things are passed away; behold, all things are become new. And all things are of God"...* II Cor. 5:17,18

We are Christ like. We are in Him, and God see us the same way He see Jesus. How can we be one with Christ, and look, talk or act differently than he does.

Wherever I go, no matter what time of the day or night it maybe, I will always look, act and talk like Phillip, because, me and Phillip are one. I can not be separated from me. And so it is, when it comes to being a new creature in Christ Jesus.

Eph. 5:1 says, *" Be ye therefore followers of God, as dear children* ... The word follower in the Greek language for this text means; **to imitate or mimic.** Therefore this scripture says we are imitate, mimic or act like our father and Jesus our Lord. We are to grow up and be carbon copies of them.

Paul said, " I'm crucified with Christ: never-theless I live; yet not I, but Christ lives in me: and the life which I now live in the flesh I live by faith in the son of God who loved me and gave himself for me."
Gal. 2:20

When I'm acting contrary to the ways of Christ I'm being a hypocrite. I know that statement kind of flips the conventional use of that word around, but for a born again, new creature in Christ, to act, think or speak differently from Jesus is hypocrisy, because you are not acting, speaking or thinking as you really are.

You may say, "but I'm just keeping it real, or being transparent, when I talk about my flaws or weak-nesses." Ok, that's cool, however, Joel 3:10 says, *"Let the weak say I'm strong."* How do you explain that command? There is but one simple way, agree with the word and say you are strong, although you may seem weak or incapable. That my friend, is keeping it real base on the truth of God's word.

God said, we are to call things which be not as though they were, not as is. When Abraham's name was changed by God, he went around declaring he was the father of a multitude, although he had not yet re-ceived the promised child. Was he lying? Was he keep-ing it real? Or was he acting like God, in whose image he was created, and calling those things which be not as though they were?

We must see ourselves the way God see and speaks of us. God says things like; we are more than conquerors, world over comers, the head and not the tail, blessed going out and coming in. We are triumphant, victorious and the gates of hell can not prevail against us.

Therefore, when you see or speak of yourself as a grasshopper, or someone who is just barely saved by grace and trying to keep the faith, you are not acting like who you really are.

The scriptures says. *"For if any being a hearer of the word, and not a doer, he is like unto a man beholding his natural face in a glass: For he beholdeth himself, and goeth his way, and straightway forgetteth what manner of man he was.* James 1:23,24.

The word of God, is described as a mirror, and if you look into that mirror, the word, and see yourself as you actually are, but then shut the bible and act and speak differently than what you read, then you are deceiving yourself, because you are not acting like the scriptures said you are.

However verse 25 says, *"But whoso looketh into the perfect law of liberty, and continueth therein, he being not a forgetful hearer, but a doer of the work, this man shall be blessed in his deed"*.

Notice, the man or woman, who sees themselves as the scripture says, and behaves as such, this person shall be blessed or empowered to prosper, and be a success in all of their deeds.

You must win, why? Because failure is not a part of your make up. We can't lose with what we use. There is no failure in Jesus, even death couldn't keep him down, therefore, there is no failure in you. Set backs, hardships and adversities can't stop you. So rise and shine for thy light has come, and glory of the Lord has risen upon You. You are in the image of Jesus.

II Cor. 3:18 says. *"But we all, with open face beholding as in a glass the glory of the Lord, are changed into the same image from glory to glory even as by the Spirit of the Lord."*

As we look into the word, we behold the glory of our Lord, however the scripture also says, we are changed into the image of his likeness or glory, by the Holy Spirit. In other words, as we feed on the word of God we are moment by moment, day by day, being changed into his image. The only way this can happen is by looking at yourself in the mirror.

There is a scene in the movie, "The Lion King," where Cymbal, The young lion, had difficulty living up to who he really was. He was living with the guilt of being responsible for his father's death, therefore, he saw himself as a failure, and felt he was unworthy to assume his position, as the next king. He lived his life as a common animal, trying to ignore, his true identity.

One day, the wise monkey led him to a body of water and encouraged him to look into it, when he did, he saw the image of his father the king, rather than himself as a failure. Of course the reflection he saw was actually the reflection of himself as a king. When he accepted what he saw, he was empowered to go back to the homeland and take his rightful place as king, and so he reigned.

Most of us are familiar with the scripture that says, *"as a man thinketh in his heart so is he."*
Pro. 23:7

But how about proverbs 27:19 which says, *"As in water face answereth face, so the heart of man to man."* This scripture is basically saying the same as proverbs 23:7, however, it adds a little something more. Notice it says, "as in water face answers face", in other words, when you look into water, you see a reflection of yourself, just as you would, when looking into a mirror. The way you see yourself, establishes what you believe in your heart about yourself. This is why the scriptures exhorts us to renew our minds with the word, so we can see ourselves and believe of ourselves the way God sees and believes of us.

Chapter 3

Mind Renewing:
Changing What You Say

Do you realize that your words govern your life?
Do you know that what you are saying today
About yourself determines where you are
Going to be tomorrow?

The Power of Words!

"A man's belly shall be satisfied with the fruit of his mouth and with the increase of his lips shall he be filled: Death and life are in the power of the tongue: and they that love it shall eat the fruit thereof" Proverbs 18:20-21

Another practice you must develop in order to renew your mind, is the controlling of your tongue. The latter part of the aforementioned scripture, plainly indicates that we have the power to speak life or death, blessings or curses. I encourage you to find out what God has said about you in His Word and then begin to affirm it or say it with your mouth. Jesus said, *"the words that I speak unto you, they are spirit, and they are life."* John 6:63. Jesus also said, *"the words I hear my father say is what I say,"* as disciples of Jesus we too must fill our mouths with the words of the father, speaking life to everything around us.

What are you constantly saying about yourself, your finances, family, business, church or any other circumstances that you're facing? Are you speaking words of doubt, fear, pain, lack or failure? Well, I want you to bear this very important fact in mind, whatever you are saying about yourself is what you are going to have in life. This is a spiritual law that none of us can escape. In the Amplified Bible, Proverbs 18:20-21 says...*"A man's moral self shall be filled with the fruit of his mouth:*

and with the <u>consequence</u> of his words he must be satisfied, whether good or evil. Death and life is in the power of the tongue, and they who indulge in it shall eat the fruit of it (for death or for life)".

Therefore, if you say that you are a failure, poor, sick, depressed, confused, etc., or if you are saying you are successful, victorious, healed, prosperous, of a sound mind, etc., then that is what you are, or will eventually become. Because the words you speak will govern your life.

In the last chapter we saw in Numbers 13:31-33, how the people of God said things with their mouths that deprived them of the enjoyment of the blessings of God which He promised them. God did not withhold the blessing from them, but they themselves, by the words of their own mouths, nullified the blessing. God told them that He <u>HAD GIVEN THEM</u> the land that flowed with milk and honey. It was a land that was very fruitful. Nevertheless, when the twelve men came back from examining the land, ten of them spoke words contrary to what God had already spoken to the people. The ten men said, they (the people of God) were unable to possess the land because of the giants that occupied it. The scripture says in verses 31-33 "but the men that went up with him said, WE BE NOT ABLE TO GO UP AGAINST THE PEOPLE; FOR THEY ARE STRONGER THEN WE. And they brought up an evil report of the land which they had searched unto the children of Israel, saying, the land, through which we have gone to search it, is a land that eateth up the inhabitants thereof; and all the people that we saw in it are men of a great stature.

And there we saw the giants, the sons of Anak, which come of the giants: AND WE WERE IN OUR OWN SIGHT AS GRASSHOPPERS, and so we were in their sight." However, the bible says *"we can do all things through Christ who strengthens us"*, and, *"all things are possible to him that believes"*. As a result of what they believed, and said of themselves, regarding that which they were facing, they died in the wilderness.

Never judge your situation from the outward appearance only, because what you see in always subject to change. But on the contrary judge them on the bases of what the scriptures says. Search out scriptures that addresses your issue, spend time meditating and rather than confessing what you see, affirm the word of God over it. You must be empowered by your faith, and not fall prey to doubt, unbelief or fear.

Remind yourself, of the very fact, that God can not lie. If you have His word on the matter, and exercises faith in the promise, then God is well able to bring it to pass, no matter what it looks like.

When Jesus got word of Lazarus' illness, he remained in the place where he was, until Lazarus died. Jesus knew that the end result, would bring glory God. To make a long story short, Jesus raised Lazarus from the grave, after he had been dead for four days.

That same power is made available to us today, therefore, how can we allow our adversary, to talk us into a mental state of hopelessness, when it is written, *"for with God ALL things are possible."* He also said *" they that trust or hope in Him, shall not be ashamed".* There is always hope, and if there is a will, there is a way.

Mark 11:23 Jesus said… *"for verily I say unto you, that whosoever shall say unto this mountain, be thou removed, and be thou cast into the sea; and shall not doubt in his heart, but shall believe that those things which he saith shall come to pass; he shall have whatsoever he saith"*…. In short, whatever you are continuously saying with your mouth, will eventually determine what you believe in your heart. When what you believe in your heart is spoken with the mouth you release supernatural power to bring it to pass. It is written, out of the abundance of that which is in your heart, you will speak and Jesus said, **if it is in your heart and you speak it with your mouth, you will have it.**

Words has the power to create, to build up and to tear down. Jesus spoke of the creative power of words in the 12th chapter of the book of Matthew. Verse 35 says, *"The good man from his inner good treasure flings forth good things, and an evil man out of his inner evil storehouse flings forth evil things.* (amplified version). The term flings forth, means to fling into existence or cause to come into be-ing. Therefore, we must be mindful to take a personal evaluation of the words that we are speaking on a daily basis over our children, our finances, our bodies, etc., because the outcome of your circumstances, even the governing of your body will be determined by the words you speak.

Go to the book of James, chapter 3; notice if you will, verses 1-6, which reads…

"My brethren, be not many masters, knowing that we shall receive the greater condemnation. For in many things we offend all. If any man offend not in word, the same is a perfect man, and able also to bridle the whole body.

Behold, we put bits in the horses' mouths, that they may obey us; and we turn about their whole body. Behold, also the ships, which though they be so great, and are driven of fierce winds, yet are they turned about with a very small helm, withersoever the governor listeth.
(Even so the tongue is a little member, and boasteth great things. Behold, how great a matter a little fire kindleth! And the tongue is a fire, a world of iniquity: so is the tongue among our members, that it defileth the whole body and setteth on fire the course of nature; and it is set on fire of hell.)"

Recently I read a book entitled "The FOURTH DIMENSION, by Dr. Paul Yonggi Cho, which referred to the power of words. He talks about how the speech center in the brain, has dominion over all the rest of the nervous system that governs the body. This in essence, is what James is also saying in this verse of scripture.

You must deposit God's word into your heart through meditation. In Chapter 4, I will show how this is done.

Depositing God's word into your heart you will enable you to develop your faith in His promises. Then, as you release your faith, by saying with your mouth, what God has said in his word, you will begin the process, of changing your life for good. But remember, in order for you to continue to walk in the blessing and goodness of God, you must hold fast to your confession, continuously saying, what God has said about you, and all that concerns you! Although, you may not see or feel an immediate change, don't give up. For your change has already begun, and you shall see it, **if you faint not!**

This process is like planting seed in the ground. When that seed is covered with soil, the law of germination begins. However, we can not see the movement or growth taking place. Jesus said.

"So is the Kingdom of God, as if a man should cast seed into the ground; and should sleep, and rise night and day, and the seed should spring and grow up, he knoweth not how. For the earth bringeth forth fruit of herself; first the blade, then the ear, after that the full corn in the ear.... Mark 4:26-28

I must reiterate this truth, that the process has begun, although, you can't see or feel it, therefore you must walk by faith not by sight or feeling.

Therefore, I encourage you to be strong, and hold fast to your confession of faith, without wavering, for God is faithful and able, to do all that He has promised, according to Hebrews 10:23

Chapter 4

Mind Renewing:
The Principles of Biblical Meditation

"This book of the Law shall not depart from your mouth,
but you shall meditate in it day and night, that you
may observe to do according to all that is written in it.
For then you will make your way prosperous, and
then you will have good success."
Joshua 1:8

The principles of biblical meditation, are very important to know, because this is how, to change the way you think, speak, and see yourself. We often say, "we need to meditate on God's word," but there is a process to meditation, that must be learned and master, if we are to meditate, properly and effectively. I will discuss two vitally important aspects of biblical meditation in this chapter. First, I will define what meditation is, and second, I will discuss, how to meditate. Unless we have proper knowledge, of the principles for meditation, or the how to, of meditation, we will not be able to receive the fullness of what God has intended, from the practice of it. Meditation, when properly practiced, will not only renew your mind, but will also develop and fortify your faith and confidence in God.

God said in the first chapter of Joshua, verse 8…

"This book of the Law shall not depart from your mouth, but you shall MEDITATE in it day and night, that you may observe to do according to all that is written in it. For then you will make your way prosperous, and then you will have good success." Also, in Psalms 1:1-3 the scripture reads,

"Blessed is the man that walketh not in the counsel of the ungodly, nor standeth in the way of sinners, nor sitteth in the seat of the scornful. But his delight is in the law of the Lord; and in his law doth he MEDITATE day and night. And he shall be like a tree planted by the rivers of water, that bringeth forth his fruit in his season; his leaf also shall not wither; and whatsoever he doeth shall prosper."

Meditating the word of God enables you to persist in doing the word, which in turn promises you prosperity and success. It is written, *"whosoever looketh into the perfect law of liberty, and continueth therein, he being not a forgetful hearer, but a doer of the work, this man shall be blessed in all his deeds."* It is one thing to read your bible, but you must put what you read to practice, allowing the word of God, by the supply of the Holy Spirit, to actually change the way you think, and subsequently, change the way you do things, this is where success begins. This is why meditation is so very important.

Now, let's define the word **"MEDITATION"** from it's Hebrew origin. The Hebrew word is pronounced: "Haw-gaw"… which means to murmur (in pleasure or anger), to ponder, to imagine, and to mutter. All of these words define the one word **"MEDITATION"**. They all have a distinct and separate part to play in the process of meditation. Therefore, we will look at each word separately, and then see how they all work collectively, to produce the effective results in our lives that we need.

The word "**murmur**" is defined in the Funk & Wagnall's Dictionary as a low, indistinct, continuous, repeated sound, also to grumble softly… Therefore, in regards to biblical meditation, murmur means to take the scriptures or a particular scripture and softly and repeatedly say it over and over again to oneself for a period of time. It is the same thing that we do when someone make us mad or upset, we murmur or grumble our displeasure, beneath our breath, so to speak.

The word **"ponder"** means; to weigh heavily in the mind, consider carefully, to reflect upon a matter. It means to think upon a phrase or statement, very carefully and continuously, that is over and over again, a good synonym for ponder is ruminate. Actually, we do quite a bit of pondering. However, we tend to ponder on the wrong things, such as our problems, whether they are financial, physical, marital etc., instead of pondering or thinking on God's word. We ponder the negatives, rather than think heavily and carefully on the positives. Philippians 4:8 says, *"finally, brethren, whatsoever things are true, whatsoever things are honest, whatsoever things are just, whatsoever things are pure, whatsoever things are lovely, whatsoever things are of good report; if there be any virtue and if there be any praise, think on, ponder, consider carefully and reflect on these things."* Paul instructs us in this verse very plainly. He is saying, we are to give our time and attention to the word of God. It is said "the mind is a terrible thing to waste. So do not waste your time or mind thinking negatively, nor should you waste your mind worrying about problems you cannot change.

If you could change a particular situation, I am sure you would have already done so, right? Give your time and attention to thinking, pondering and reflecting on the promises of God. Do not allow the devil to cause mental torment in your mind, by magnifying your problems. Keep in mind, the solution to every problem, is already in the word of God. Seek out the promises and then meditate on them continuously. Murmur and ponder the word, not the problem.

In connection to murmuring, you must also take time to ponder, which means, to think heavily upon, over and over again, ruminating the same scripture(s) that you have been murmuring during this period of meditation. These two work together in the meditation process, yet each is separate and distinct in itself.

The word **"imagine,"** means to form a mental picture of something in your mind; it is to conceive, or create in the mind a clear picture of a person, place, desire, or thing. This principle of biblical meditation, I think, is the most difficult. Because to imagine, we must create the images intentionally. Although, it is something that we do very often, nevertheless, most of the images we see, just kind of, floated into our minds, so to speak. And the majority of them are negative.

When it comes to the usage of your imagination during meditation, you must form a mental picture of yourself, or your circumstances, in agreement with what the scriptures says concerning you. For example, let's say that you are believing God for healing, then you should gather together the scriptures that pertain to healing. Such as, Isaiah 53:5, Psalms 103.3 and 1 Peter 2:24, just to name a few.

All of these scriptures, are like medicine for your flesh, which God has provided.

Pro. 4:22 says, *"for they are life to those that find them and health to all their flesh.*

The word health, in that text is translated medicine. Just as you would take your natural medicine, prescribed by your Dr., you must also take your supernatural medication prescribed by the **Lord Who Healeth Us**, through the process of meditation.

I remembered once having chest pain, accompanied by gradual fatigue. If went on for several days, with no relief. One even, while laying across the bed, the Holy Spirit instructed me, to spend some time meditating on the healing scriptures. So I did. I would read the verse out loud, then lay back, and meditate on it, using the methods I'm writing about in this book. After meditating awhile, I repeat the process. I did it three times. However, after the third time, I heard the Holy Spirit say to me, "you are healed", then I felt gentle breeze flow across my body, and I fell off to sleep. I awoke the next day, and took my two nephews to the park, and played basketball with them .

After you have given time to murmuring and pondering the scriptures, you must use your imagination to form a mental picture of yourself healed and well. You must come to the place where you see yourself healed. You have to see yourself well. You have to have a mental picture of yourself out of bed, full of energy and life.

Do not allow a picture of sickness, bedridden or death to stay in your mind, not for one second. You must cast down negative images, and use your imagination, to see yourself in line with God's word. We will go over this particular principle further in chapter 5.

There is one other principle that we must practice, in order to thoroughly meditate the way God intended. It is the process of **"muttering".** Muttering is somewhat similar to murmuring. However, when you mutter, you are speaking in a very low voice, such as to whisper to one self, over and over again. In essence, you are talking to yourself. Of course, there isn't anything wrong with that. David himself said, *"Bless the Lord O my soul and forget not all His benefits.":* Well, who do you think David is talking to in that passage of scripture? That's right, he is telling his soul, to bless the Lord, and not to forget His benefits! We too, need to do that sometimes. Rather then complaining or worrying, we need to say to our souls, **SOUL, STOP COMPLAINING AND WORRYING AND BLESS THE LORD FOR HIS GOODNESS!!** Then we should begin to praise God for all of His benefits which He has already provided us. I tell you, if you will do this, the peace of God will supernaturally, flood your mind and cause fear and worry to flee far from you.

Remember, meditation means to **murmur,** or **mutter** to *ponder,* and to **imagine.** All of which is to be done in one sitting, if you are going to complete the full process of meditation.

I personally think, the order that you do this is also vitally important. Although the order that you choose to do them is totally left up to you. However, you must do them all to complete the overall process of meditation.

In my time of meditation, the first thing that I do is murmur or mutter the scriptures. I do this first, so that I can focus my mind or give my full attention to these scriptures. Because normally, when you are saying something, it is coming through your mind. Therefore, I'm thinking and saying the same thing. Thereby, I'm intentional blocking out all other thoughts at that time. It is easy to ponder the scripture from this point because my mind is already focused. So I simply ponder quietly on the same scriptures for a while. Then I begin to use my imagination to form my mental picture, concluding with thanksgiving to God for the results.

I know for a fact, as you put these principles together and practice them on a consistent basis, you will definitely see a great change in your life. Regardless to what you to change, god's word, when meditated upon, will bring about the desired end. Which is success, victory and prosperity.

Chapter 5

Breaking Stubborn Habits Through Biblical Meditation

"All things are lawful unto me, but all things are not expedient: all things are lawful for me, but I will not be brought under the power of any"

1Corinthians 6:12

Paul said that all things are lawful for him, but all things are not expedient or good for him. Again he says, although all things may be lawful for him, yet **he will not allow** himself to become

Paul said, "all things are lawful for him", but all things are not expedient or good for me. Again he says, "although all things may be lawful for him, yet **he will not allow** himself to become enslaved to, or practice anything that would hinder him, from succeeding in the call of God upon his life. Nor will he allow, any type of self sabotaging habit, to hinder him from living successfully, in any other area of his life.

Heb. 12:1   says, ..."*let us lay aside every weight , and the sin which doth so easily beset us, and let us run with patience the race that is set before us".*
The word weight means, encumbrance, or something that weighs or slow us downs. Something that hinders us from achieving the desired end.

When runners are competing , they don't wear a jacket or boots, do they? No, they have on the lightest clothing possible, so they can run swiftly, and without any unnecessary weight.

Paul also said, *"Know ye not, that they that run in a race run all, but one receiveth the prize? So run that ye may obtain. And every man that striveth for the mastery, is temperate in all things... I therefore, so run, not as uncertainly; so fight I, not as one who beateth the air: But I keep my body under and bring it into subjection...*

He is talking about, the importance of developing and maintaining self control. He was conscious of practicing good productive habits, so he could be, have and do all he can, while on this earth. So should we think and strive for the same.

Habit is defined as, a behavior pattern acquired and fixed by frequent repetition. We could have good habits that work positively for us, whereas on the contrary, we could also have bad habits that work against our well being. The habits may not always be sinful, according to the way we define sin. These may be habits that doesn't benefit or contribute to a productive lifestyle for ourselves or others. For instance, let's say you have a bad habit of starting projects and quitting before you complete them. Or, suppose you are one who tend to procrastinate or put off for tomorrow, what you could or should do today. We could also name many other habits that are not beneficial, such as biting your fingernails, over eating, or excessively talking, of course there are many, many more.

I mentioned earlier, concerning people who yet struggle with habits, such as, cigarette smoking, drunkeness, drug abuse, excessive or unnatural sexual desires, such as homosexuality and lesbianism, just to name a few. These are not sinful behaviors produced as a primary result of, or because of, demonic influence. The main reason for these patterns of behavior, can be attributed to mental bondage. Some people may say that these patterns of behavior are only the result of demons. This is true, to a certain extent. For all sin, or temptation to sin, is demonically influenced. But we must also realize, the important fact that habits are also the result of one's own will.

We must also recognize it as a mental thing, being in bondage to behave in such ways. Remember, Paul said for us to present our bodies, that is, to discipline our bodies and bring it into subjection, to the Word of God. We are to renew our minds, so that we are not dictated or motivated, by the world system which is governed by Satan.

Romans 12:1-2 says *"I beseech you therefore, brethern, by the mercies of God, that you present your bodies a living sacrifice, holy, acceptable unto God, which is your reasonable service. And be not conformed to this world: but be ye transformed, by the renewing of your mind, that you may prove what is that good, and acceptable, and perfect will of God."* (Romans 12:1-2).

The Word of God tells us that Satan is seeking whom he may devour, that is, to destroy. However, do not allow him to devour you through deception. Don't allow him to deceive you to believe that your problem or habit is something that you must endure for the rest of your life, because this is not so.

He's a liar and the truth is not in him. If you put the following principles of Mind Renewal to work in the areas of your life, where you have habits that you need and desire to change, then you will surely be triumphant and victorious over them.

Now, the principles of mind renewal works like this; you must first of all identify what it is you desire to change about yourself.

Then, you must establish a foundation for the change through the Word of God. For example, if the scripture says, **you can do all things through Christ, who is your strength,** according to Philippians 4:13, then this could be your scriptural foundation that could produce the faith and spiritual strength that's needed to put you over, and cause you to be more than a conqueror as God has said! In Isaiah 55:11. God said His Word which He has spoken concerning you will not return unto Him void of doing that which He purposed. Nor will it return to Him without producing in you the results that He has promised. It is just a matter of you taking His Word and putting it into your heart and renewing your mind with it. Begin to put the principles of meditation to practice as we defined and discussed earlier. In review, meditation means to **"mutter"** or to speak softly as to one's self, over and over again. It means to "ponder" or to weigh heavily on one's mind repetitiously. It means to "imagine" or to form a mental picture of something and to play it out in your mind.

Meditation is most effective when it is done approximately ten to fifteen minutes, two to three times per day. It is essential to have a quiet place to retreat to, where you will not be disturbed. Once you are in that quiet place, sit comfortably, take several deep breaths, releasing them slowly to relax. Then intentionally, free your mind of all thoughts that do not pertain to what you are about to meditate on. I call this a "shutting down of the mind", because, you are shutting down your consciousness.

You are shutting down the part of you that is aware of one's self and surroundings and opening up your subconscious (that portion of mental activity not directly in the focus of consciousness but is susceptible to recall by the proper stimulus).

This is where the desired change will have to take place first of all, in order for the change to be manifested on the outside or in your behavior. Because you have thought or behaved in such a way for so long, the practice has become impressed on the subconscience mind which is connected to or works together with your inner self, or should I say the real you. Because of this the habit is like second nature, it is something you find yourself doing without giving it any thought.

To be governed by your conscious mind, is the same as being governed by what you see, feel or hear. (the awareness of one's own existence, feelings and thoughts, external objects and conditions; being mentally awake, felt by one's self, internally known; awareness of guilt or fault and shortcomings): Whereas, to be governed by your sub-conscious mind, which is the same as your spirit, or inner self, where God's Word is planted, means to be governed by the Word of God, regardless to what you see, feel or hear. Enabling you to walk in the Spirit and not according to the flesh or the old nature, where the habit lies. You are now a new creature in Christ, you are born again, and your old nature no longer has dominion or dominance over you. The old man can only have dominion in your life if you allow it to do so.

Now you're ready to begin the process of meditation to break any stubborn habit. Take the scriptures you have chosen and begin to mutter them, speak them softly to yourself, over and over again. One of two very important things are happening here.

First, you are beginning to change what you've been saying about yourself, you're starting to agree with that which God has said about you. Second, you are now changing what you're believing about yourself, to what God believes about you. After a few moments of this, begin to ponder, that is, to think heavily on what the scriptures, particularly the ones you have chosen, are saying concerning you. One of the main benefits that come from pondering the Word of God is stated in Mark 4:24, which says,

"take heed to what you hear: with what measure you mete, it shall be measured to you: and unto you that hear, shall more be given" (KJV). The Amplified Bible says it this way,

"And He said to them be careful what you are hearing. The measure (of thought and study) you give (to the truth you hear) will be the measure (of virtue and knowledge) that comes back to you and more (besides) will be given to you who hear."

The measure of thought and study you give to a particular scripture is the same as pondering or thinking heavily on it; which will cause you to receive revelation and increased knowledge of the scriptures you are giving your attention to.

After a time of pondering, it is now time for the fun part! Which is, to imagine or the forming of a mental picture of yourself that is in agreement with

God's Word. See yourself in a way that is in agreement with God. See yourself delivered and free of every habit that hinders your from developing into a mature Christian.

The scriptures says in Romans 6:11, *"Likewise reckon yourself to be dead indeed unto sin, but alive unto God through Jesus Christ our Lord"*.
The word **reckon,** means to consider a thing to be so. Paul is saying we are to, by faith, consider or acknowledge ourselves to dead to our sin nature, and alive unto God or godliness.

My greatest struggle, after I was born again, was with an old habit, of viewing porn, which I picked up at the age of nine. I would constantly cry out to God in prayer, asking Him for help and deliverance. Only to have him respond to me each time with the following words, **"I Have Already Helped You."**

I went on a fast that lasted approximately forty days, in an attempt to break the habit or overcome the bondage. During the fast, my mother informed me, that a highly spoken of, and anointed man of God, was coming to town, and suggested, I should go and have him pray for me, which I agreed to.

I was the first one to get to the meeting place, and the first in the building. I eagerly sat through the service, anxiously awaiting the alter call. When that moment came. I was front and center. The Minister laid hands on us one at a time, this was a pentecostal kind of a meeting, therefore shouting or praising God, in a highly emotional dance, was common place.

One person after the other, would breakout in a dance as he prayed for them. As he approached me, my anticipation level must have been to the ceiling by now, I knew when he laid hands on me, the power, or the anointing of God, was going to instantly set me free.

I stood there, with my hands raised in the presence of the Lord, when suddenly he touched me, uttered a few words and went on to the next person. All I felt, was disappointment, **No Shake, No rattle, Nor roll,** just has hand. I felt Cheated or passed over. With my hands still lifted, I heard the Lord ask me this question, **"what are you doing here?'** I immediately and emphatically responded, **"Lord you know why I'm here!"** He said to me, **"go home and break your fast."** While the man of God was still praying for others, I stepped out of the line, and exited the building, for I had heard from the Lord.

I stopped by a Circle K gas station, and bought two hot dogs and a grape soda, boy was I glad to end that fast..

Shortly afterward, the Holy Spirit started teaching me these very principles and practices, I'm sharing with you now.   At one point, I believed I was in bondage, however, after practicing meditation, my belief changed, and I knew I was free.

You may ask the question, well, did you view pornography any more after that. The answer is yes, however, it wasn't because I was believed I was enslaved by it any longer, but because, I simply chose to view it. But now I was deliberately, disobeying God, because the Holy Spirit had revealed to me the truth.

God made it very clear to me, what I had to do. He gave me the understanding, that I had a responsibility to walk in my liberty, my victory and my deliverance. I had to renew my mind to the fact that **HE HAD ALREADY DELIVERED ME.** I had to meditate on that truth, until my belief changed from being in bondage, to I'm delivered.

Do you remember why the people of God could not enter the promise land? It was because they would not believe God's word. God said the land is yours, they said we can't do it. He said I have given you the land, they said we are not able. God said, well ok, if you won't believe me, then I can't help you, and the only other option, is to die in the wilderness. Which is exactly what happened, all because they would not believe.

Many times due to a lack of knowledge, Christians continue to live their lives according to the old nature. They continue in the old habits because they have not come to a place of embracing the true fact that they are now **NEW CREATURES** in Christ. It is apparent, many Christians fail to walk in this newness of life because they have not come to a place of having renewed their mind pertaining to their new life in Christ. That's why we are instructed in Romans 12:1-2, to renew our minds and we are to present our own bodies a living sacrifice unto God by faith. As we do this or as we embrace these facts, among many others, we will begin to walk in the deliverance and victory that God has already given us.

As God began to teach me about the principles of meditation, one of the scriptures that I would primarily meditate on was, Galatians 2:20, which reads, "I am crucified with Christ, nevertheless I live, yet not I, but Christ that lives within me...": I would mutter and ponder this verse, over and over again all during the day, for many days. Then, when I came to the principle of imagining, I would form a mental picture of myself hanging on a cross, the old me. I would imagine the old me that was habitually bound, now crucified; I would see the old me, now dead to that particular lifestyle. By doing this, I was renewing my mind to the fact that I was a new creature in Christ in that area of my life. What I was now seeing regularly and focusing my attention on, was producing a new image of myself, within my subconscious mind. This enabled me to walk free from the old habit.

Observation, or what you are constantly seeing has a lot to do with strongholds that will develop in the subconscious mind, as well as, what you believe.

Notice what happened to Lot, as a result of dwelling among the wicked, observing and listing to their filthy conduct and conversation…(For that righteous man dwelling among them, in seeing and hearing, vexed his righteous soul from day to day with their unlawful deeds.) Lot was a righteous man, nevertheless the scriptures says, his soul was vexed. In other words, he was mentally oppressed by what he gave his attention to from day to day.

Hebrews 11:1 says… *"Now, faith is the substance of things hoped for, the evidence of things not seen…"* Faith is the evidence of the things not yet seen in the natural realm, however, in itself, faith does see something. Faith perceives the things that you are hoping for by a mental picture having been developed in the mind, mainly through and in your time of meditation. It is said that, if you can conceive it, then you can believe it.

In line with what we are discussing here, let us take a moment to consider what it means to conceive within the mind. It means, **to form in the mind; to develop mentally a clear picture of that which you desire to be;** This is the hope that faith gives substance to. You see, if you can not see it by faith, then you do not give faith anything to work with on your behalf.

Notice Hebrews 11:13 says, *"these all died in faith, not having received the promises, but having seen them afar off, and were persuaded of them, and embraced them, and confessed that they were strangers and pilgrims on the earth"*. Although they did not receive the promises before they died, they did see them. What they saw was conceived in their mind first, (through, what I believe was meditation) which eventually entered into their spirits. What they saw was so real to them, they became fully persuaded of that which God had promised, to a place of being able to embrace them by faith.

It is vitally important to guard your mind. Remember, the mind is the center of all bodily activity. It is within the mind that strongholds begin, thereby, taking control of the body's behavior. This is how a habit is formed. If the mind is changed, then so will a change of behavior take place. Once this takes place, habits are broken. Paul said in IICorinthians 10:4-5...

"for the weapons of our warfare are not carnal, but mighty through God to the pulling down of STRONGHOLDS; casting down IMAGINATIONS, and every high thing that exalteth itself against the knowledge of God, and bringing into captivity EVERY THOUGHT to the obedience of Christ".

Now, once again, create in your mind, during your time of meditation, images or mental pictures of the way you want it (that is, whatever it is that you desire) to be and not the way that it currently is. Mentally see yourself free, healed, prosperous, victorious, blessed and abounding in the work of the Lord. Now, begin to praise God and say with your mouth that YOU ARE free; YOU ARE healed; YOU ARE prosperous; YOU ARE victorious, blessed and abounding in the work of the Lord. You are who the word says you are, no matter what the situation appears to be.

Not because of what you see in the natural, but BECAUSE OF WHAT YOU CONCEIVE WITHIN YOUR MIND AND BELIEVE IN YOUR HEART. Again, remember, it is said that if you can conceive it, then you can believe it, and if you can believe it and confess it, then you will possess it.

Chapter 6

Calling Those Things
That Be Not
As Though They Are

One day I was just going along minding my own business, when the Holy Spirit said these words to me, "there is a difference between the act of muttering and confessing"; He went on to say, "when you are muttering, you are causing those words to fill your spirit to establish and or fortify your belief. Whereas, on the other hand, when you confess, or make a bold affirmation, of those things you believe in your heart, you are releasing the faith it takes to bring what you believe to pass.

You are releasing the Power of God into the Spirit realm, causing an effect, to bring to pass, in the natural realm, those things that He has promised in the words you were muttering. It may sound complicated, but it is quite simple. That is why I believe the scriptures encourage us "NOT TO LEAN TO OUR OWN UNDERSTANDING", because the things of God are simple, yet we tend to complicate them, when we try to reason them out for ourselves or within ourselves.

The word of God, is fulfilled in our lives, by this simple principle; Believe in your heart and confess with your mouth or, by the speaking of FAITH FILLED WORDS. Whenever we speak words that are filled with faith, the Holy Spirit (who is the third person of the Godhead) by those words we've spoken, begin to tear down, pull down, destroy, build up and or bring to pass what we are saying in faith. Notice, if you will, Genesis 1:1-3 says...

"In the beginning God created the heaven and the earth. And the earth was without form and void;

and darkness was upon the face of the deep. And the Spirit of God moved upon the face of the waters. And God said, let there be light: and there was light."

Notice, while the earth was without form and void and darkness was all around, the scripture says that the Spirit of God moved upon the face of the waters. Now the Spirit of God and the power of God are one in the same, so we can say, although the power of God was present to cause a change, there was no change, until God spoke faith filled words. Notice if you will, when God said, "LET THERE BE LIGHT", it was then that the Holy Spirit, or the power of God, began to move to create light in the earth. Jesus said, *"the words that I speak are spirit and life"*.

In Hebrews 4:12 Paul said, *"the Word of God is alive and powerful"*...again in the book of Ephesians 4:17, Paul also says, *"the Word of God is the sword of the Spirit."*

Now, consider what I am about to share with you very carefully. The Word of God without the Spirit is lifeless, because it is the Spirit that gives the Word of God life. And the Spirit Himself cannot do anything without the spoken Word of God. Therefore, these two forces must be in operation together in order to bring into manifestation what God wants.

The spoken Word of God is the sword or the instrument, by which the Holy Spirit uses to create or to tear down. When Jesus spoke to the fig tree, saying *"no man eat fruit of thee hereafter forever"*, it was the power of the Holy Spirit, working through those faith filled words, He spoke, that caused the fig tree to rot from the roots.

It was the Holy Spirit operating through the faith filled words of Jesus, that drove the demons and sickness from the bodies of the people He ministered to. It will also be by, faith filled words, spoken from your mouth, that will activate the Holy Spirit, to perform in your body and or circumstances.

Therefore, let's go back to where we started, remembering, before you start to confess the Word of God, to release the power, you must give yourself time of meditation first. This will establish your belief or the convictions of your heart. The heart that I am referring to, is the inner being or the Spirit of man. Proverbs 18:20 calls it the "belly", it reads,

"A MAN'S BELLY SHALL BE SATISFIED WITH THE FRUIT OF HIS MOUTH; AND WITH THE INCREASE OF HIS LIPS SHALL HE BE FILLED".

Notice, it says, the man's belly, his spirit or his heart, shall be satisfied, by what comes out of his mouth, and shall be filled by the increase of what he is saying. As I have said before, I say again, this is where muttering and confessing differ. Remember, muttering is for your hearing and filling. Whereas, confessing is a releasing of that which you are filled with. You must get filled and then speak, in order to release and produce. Jesus said,
\

"It is out of the abundance (or overflow) of that which is in the heart that a man speaks and brings forth (or causes to be)."

When we declare the word of God, that is, make a bold affirmation of our beliefs or convictions, which is based on God's word, we must speak in present tense terminology, as if it is already done.

Whenever God gives a promise, it as already settled, as far as, He is concern. Ps. 119:89 says,
"for ever, O' Lord, thy word is settled in heaven. Thy faithfulness is unto all generations: thou hath established the earth, and it abideth."

We don't have to question him about them, according to II Cor. 1:20,
"For all the promises of God in Him are yea (yes), and in Him Amen, (so be it) unto the glory of God by us."

If we are going to walk with God, we must agree with Him, (not him with us, but we with Him) For how can two walk together unless they agree.

We should be saying the same things God has said, and say them as though they are done.

II Cor. 4:13 says,
"We having the same spirit of faith according as it is written, I believe and therefore have I spoken, we also believe and therefore speak."

We believe the word, and therefore speak it.

Abraham called himself, what God called him. God said to Abraham, "you are the family of a multitude." Abraham agreed with God and called himself, the same, despite the circumstances. We too must practice calling ourselves what God calls us, even if it be not in the natural.

If God calls you healed, call yourself healed; if He calls you prosperous, declare the same over yourself; if the word says you are more than a conqueror, affirm it with your own mouth; if He calls you blessed, then talk and act like you are blessed.

Agree with God, believe and speak His word, and He will do exceeding, abundantly, above all you can ask or think. For it is written in Ephesians 3:20,

"now unto him that is able to do exceedingly abundantly above all that we ask or think, according to the power that worketh in us."

In order for God to show Himself strong on your behalf, His WORD must be in your heart and in your mouth. For this is how that same power, that raised Jesus from the dead, will operate for you, enabling you to live a victorious life through a renewed mind.

Be Fruitful & Multiply

Summary
&
Overview

4 Steps To
Renewing The Mind

Summary

Establish Foundation For Change
(Through the Word of God)

Scripture References
Isaiah 55:11   Jeremiah 1:12   Hebrews 4:12

Change What You Are Saying By Way Of Meditation
(Particularly Muttering)

Change What You Are Seeing By Way Of Meditation
(Particularly Imagining)

Scripture References
2 Peter 2:7,8   2 Corinthians 10:3-5

Call Those Things That Be Not As Though They Are

Scripture References
2 Corinthians 4:13   Mark 11:23

Now, thank God for what He has already done, not going to do!

Notes

Notes

Notes

Notes

Notes

Notes

Statement of Faith

We believe the Bible is inspired by the Holy Spirit, the infallible revelation of God to man. *II Tim.3:16-17, II Pet.1:20-21*

We believe there is only one true, eternal God revealed in three persons; Father, Son, and Holy Spirit. *Gen.1:1, 26, Deut.6:4, Isa.43:10-11, Mt.28:19*

We believe in the deity and humanity of Jesus Christ, His virgin birth, sinless life, sacrificial death to save us from our sins, and His resurrection and ascension to heaven. *Matt.1:21, 23, John 1:1-2, 14, 3:16, Acts 1:2-3, 9, 2:22*

We believe in the sinfulness of all mankind and the need of salvation, available only through the blood of Jesus Christ to all who will believe and receive Him as Savior. *Rom.3:23, 6:23, 10:13, Ephesians 2:8-9, Titus 3:4-7*

We believe the finished work of Christ on the cross provides healing for the human body. *Isa.53:4-5, Mt. 8:16-17, I Pet.2:24, James 5:14-15*

We believe in the sanctifying power of the Holy Spirit by whose indwelling, the believer is enabled to live a holy life. Sanctification is the process of being separated from sin and dedicated to God, which begins at salvation and continues throughout the lifetime of the believer. *Gal.5:22-23, I Thess.4:3-5, 5:23, II Pet.3:18*

We believe in the baptism of the Holy Spirit which is promised to all Believers subsequent to salvation as the entrance into a Spirit-filled life including: a prayer language (speaking in tongues), gifts of the Holy Spirit, and power to be a witness and anointed servant of God. *Joel 2:28-29, Lk.3:16, Acts 1:4-5, 8, 2:4, 38-39, 10:44-47, I Cor.12:4-11*

We believe in the personal, imminent return of Jesus Christ. *Acts 1:11, I Thess. 4:16-18, Titus 2:13*

We believe in the bodily resurrection of both the saved and the unsaved; the saved to everlasting life and the unsaved to everlasting damnation. *Acts 24:15, I Cor.15:20-23, Rev.20:4-6, 12-15*

We believe in the responsibility of every believer to reach the world with the gospel of Jesus Christ. *Mt.28:19-20, Mk.16:15-20, Acts 1:8, 2:40-41,47*

Are you Born Again? Not sure. Do you want to be Born Again or certain of it?

Do You Believe Jesus is the son of God?
Do you believe He died for your sin?
Do you believe God raised him from the dead?
Do you believe he is alive today, seated at the right hand of God?

If yes to these questions, then pray this prayer:

Dear God,

     I ask you to forgive me of my sin. I realize I need to give my life and heart to Jesus, so I can be forgiven, saved and receive eternal life. I believe Jesus is your Son, who died for my sin. I believe you raised Him from the dead, and now I confess with my mouth, Jesus is Lord of all.

     Jesus, come into my heart. Make me new in the sight of God. Save me and be Lord of my life. I thank you now! I believe you have heard me. I believe, God has received me as His child, and He has forgiven and cleansed me of all sin, I am now born again. I am now a child of God. In Jesus name, I am saved. Thank you Father for saving me. Amen!

**EMPOWERED TO BE A VOICE
NOT AN ECHO**

**PUBLISHED BY
TAKE CHARGE ENTERPRISE**
P.O. BOX 25743, COLUMBIA,
(803) 348-088

can be ob
.com
9
3/1669/P

EMPOWERED TO BE A VOICE
NOT AN ECHO

PUBLISHED BY
TAKE CHARGE ENTERPRISES, INC.
P.O. BOX 25743, COLUMBIA, SC 29224
(803) 348-0882

$9.95

ISBN 1-4243-0321-4

CPSIA information can be obtained
at www.ICGtesting.com
Printed in the USA
BVHW072352201119
564382BV00025B/1669/P